WE, THE PEOPLE OF THE UNITED STATES,

IN ORDER TO FORM A MORE PERFECT UNION,

ESTABLISH JUSTICE, INSURE DOMESTIC TRANQUILITY,

PROVIDE FOR THE COMMON DEFENSE,

PROMOTE THE GENERAL WELFARE,

AND SECURE THE BLESSINGS OF LIBERTY

TO OURSELVES AND OUR POSTERITY,

DO ORDAIN AND ESTABLISH THIS

CONSTITUTION FOR THE

UNITED STATES OF AMERICA.

BEFORE HE ENTER ON THE EXECUTION OF HIS OFFICE,

HE SHALL TAKE THE FOLLOWING OATH OR AFFIRMATION:

"I DO SOLEMNLY SWEAR THAT I WILL FAITHFULLY EXECUTE

THE OFFICE OF PRESIDENT OF THE UNITED STATES,

AND WILL TO THE BEST OF MY ABILITY,

PRESERVE, PROTECT AND DEFEND

THE CONSTITUTION OF THE UNITED STATES."

An American Journey

BUILDING A BRIDGE TO THE 21ST CENTURY

MATTHEW NAYTHONS

PRODUCER

DAWN SHEGGEBY

EDITOR

ACEY HARPER

DIRECTOR OF PHOTOGRAPHY

ALEX CASTRO

ART DIRECTOR

AN EPICENTER COMMUNICATIONS BOOK

Photographs: previous page, Galen Rowell; this page, Acey Harper

The U.S. Capitol towers over the landscape
in this drawing commemorating the
inauguration of Rutherford Hayes in 1877.
The Washington Monument (16) stands
incomplete in the background, a stump of
concrete that would not soar to its present
height of 555 feet, 5 1/8 inches until 1886.

Photograph: Library of Congress

Producer: Matthew Naythons

Project Director and Editor: Dawn Sheggeby
Director of Photography: Acey Harper
Art Director: Alex Castro

Assistant Editor: Kylen Campbell

Associate Art Director: Ingrid Castro

Captions: B. J. O'Kelly

Photo Editors:
    Barbara Nugent
    Robin Bowman
    Barbara Ries
    Saba Press Photos

Photo Trafficking:
    Jo Jo Whilden
    Shonquis Moreno

Logistics Liaison: Rey Post

Epicenter Communications:
    President: Matthew Naythons
    VP, Associate Publisher: Peter Goggin
    VP, Art Director: Alex Castro
    Director of Operations: Martyn Harmon
    Editorial Assistant: Nancy Opitz

Epicenter Communications, Inc.
180 Harbor Drive, Suite 215
Sausalito, California, 94965
staff@epicenter.com

Printed in the United States of America
First printing: March, 1997

10 9 8 7 6 5 4 3 2 1

Foreword

KEN BURNS

John Adams never stuck around to see the inauguration of his old friend Thomas Jefferson. The bitterly contested election of 1800 that had ended Adams' presidency was too difficult a pill for him to swallow, and after naming judges sympathetic to his Federalist philosophy and guaranteed to cause trouble for the reticent republican from Virginia, crusty old John Adams—even he called himself "obnoxious"—left town before dawn rather than shake the hand of the man he had once admired enough to entrust with the writing of the Declaration of Independence, but who was now his sworn political enemy.

It had been the dirtiest election in American history, each side savaging the others in the press. When the electoral college met in the brand new capital called "Washington's City," none of the four candidates had enough votes to win. The House of Representatives would have to settle things. Congressional voting went on for six sleepless days and 36 separate ballots. They were so hopelessly deadlocked that many feared that the American experiment was failing. Finally, Alexander Hamilton urged his fellow Federalists to support his long-time philosophical rival, and the exhausted legislators eventually elected Thomas Jefferson the third president of the United States.

It was a close call. Though Adams himself had quietly gained the presidency four years before when George Washington heroically stepped down after two terms, never before in the history of the world had there been a peaceful change of governments between two such

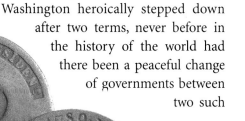

opposing parties, with such differing philosophies. For a time, it had looked as if we too would descend into bloody revolution and chaos. Indeed, the pro-Jefferson governors of Pennsylvania and Virginia had threatened to send their militias to seize the capital if the Federalists refused to accept a Jefferson victory. But it didn't happen. Instead, we would miraculously encode into the DNA of our body politic what has become the envy of every other nation on earth: the orderly, indeed sacred, transfer of power.

Soon after the crisis passed, Jefferson himself wrote that the recent events "bespeak a strength of character in our nation which augers well for the durations of the Republic; and I am much better satisfied now of its stability than I was before it was tried."

History is medicine. There is a kind of comfort in the past. It is a healing force for those who would risk a few moments of reflection and investigation. And there can be no more effective cure for our ever-changing political ailments than that marvelous ongoing pageant that we call inauguration day. The second inauguration of William Jefferson Clinton marks the continuation of this spirit into the 21st century, drawing our collective attention to the importance of history and the profundity of the event. Though we are justifiably proud of the stirring rhetoric that has often attended to this day—and some of the best American writing ever has gone forth on this day—we can take even more intense pride in the longest uninterrupted succession of freely elected governments in human history. It is our rhythm of renewal, our great gift to the rest of humanity.

Though inaugurations usually take place on some of the coldest days of the year, they nonetheless represent no less than an American Spring, where the chilliness of partisanship and political process meet the irrefutable fact of democratic rebirth. Even the scrooges of cynicism stop and take notice, and among them is a begrudging sense of what the rest of us exalt each inauguration day: that though our system is not without glaring faults we are

6

Inaugural souvenirs go back to 1789 (*far left*), when George Washington took the oath as the nation's first president in what was then the capital of the United States, New York City. Because Congress couldn't establish a quorum until April 6 to officially certify the results of the electoral college—a formality, since the Revolutionary War hero ran unopposed—the actual ceremony took place almost two months later than the scheduled date of March 4. Thomas Jefferson, the nation's third president, was the first to be inaugurated in the new capital on the Potomac. A banner declaring the political demise of his predecessor ("John Adams is no more") and a snuff box with his likeness were among the keepsakes used to celebrate his ascendancy in 1801.

Photographs: Eric F. Long, National Museum of American History, Smithsonian Institution

indeed enjoying, like no where else on earth, the blessings of liberty. It is an unusually moving moment.

We say every four years that we have invested in the cherished symbolism of the office and not in the cult of personality that attends its occupant. We invest in the liberation that comes from the avoidance of tyranny, not in the corrupting accumulation of power that attends to every coronation. We invest in the future, not in the past. Blessedly lacking in an officially sanctioned religion, we have substituted instead our civic culture, and in so doing have enshrined this day with all the symbolism of ritual. There can be no day more sacred in a democracy than the day ordinary citizens gather to watch a fellow citizen assume the heavy burden of leadership, content in the knowledge that soon that citizen will be peacefully replaced with another.

In his transcendent Declaration of Independence, Thomas Jefferson could have followed the British philosopher John Locke and said "life, liberty, and property." Instead, he left us with a miraculous legacy of restless search when he instead substituted the phrase "the pursuit of happiness." That has made all the difference for us. Most other societies have seen themselves as an end unto themselves. We Americans still quest, relentlessly. Not for a hedonistic pursuit of happiness in the marketplace of things, but for a continuing evolution of the mind and heart in the marketplace of ideas. This is our journey, the American Journey, and no other event reminds us more of the genius of our system and our remarkable ability to reinvent ourselves than does each glorious inauguration day.

Many years after that fateful inauguration, Jefferson and Adams became friends again, putting aside the differences that had strained their friendship for so long. These two old men, who were destined to die within hours of each other on the fiftieth anniversary of the day they signed the Declaration, began in the sunset of their lives a beautiful and elegiac correspondence, perhaps the greatest correspondence between public figures in American history. In one of the letters, Jefferson wrote to Adams this wonderfully moving passage:

"And so we have gone on, and so shall we go on, puzzled and prospering beyond example in the history of man. And I do believe we shall continue to grow, to multiply and prosper until we exhibit an association, powerful, wise and happy, beyond what has yet been seen [by men]. . . . I like the dreams of the future better than the history of the past. So good night. I will dream on, always fancying that Mrs. Adams and yourself are by my side marking our progress. . . ."

Bill Clinton knows something, too, about the dreams of the future, and as we approach the daunting challenges and exquisite possibilities of a new millennium, it is helpful to be guided by the powerful wisdom of our past experience, while never forgetting, as Jefferson reminds us, that that reflection must always push us forward.

KEN BURNS
Walpole, New Hampshire

The first inauguration recorded by photography was that of James Buchanan, Democrat of Pennsylvania, in 1857. James Monroe had begun the tradition of taking the oath outside the Capitol four decades earlier, and the public had enthusiastically taken to the spectacle of a peaceful transition of power: more than 100,000 people attended Buchanan's inauguration ceremony and the subsequent parade down Pennsylvania Avenue.

Photograph: National Museum of American History, Smithsonian Institution

With the rickety Capitol dome under reconstruction, and the unstable nation of the verge of disintegration, Abraham Lincoln is sworn in for his first term as president on March 4, 1861 (*left*). Since his election, seven Southern states had seceded from the United States, and the flag of the Confederate States of America flew within sight of the Capitol. The city of Washington rippled with tension on inauguration day, and extraordinary security was put in place to protect the new president. "The moment-ous issue of civil war," Lincoln said in his inaugural address, "is in your hands." That war erupted on April 12, when the Confederates fired on Fort Sumter. Five weeks after Lincoln's second inauguration (*below*), the Civil War ended; five days later, he became the first American president to die at the hands of an assassin.

Photographs: National Museum of American History, Smithsonian Institution

The bridge between two centuries, William McKinley was the last president to be inaugurated in the 19th century (*lower left,* being escorted by outgoing president Grover Cleveland) and the first to be inaugurated in the 20th (*upper left*). The program celebrating his inauguration 100 years ago (*right*) took no notice of the fact that that it would be the first swearing-in to be recorded by a newfangled invention, the motion picture camera.

Photographs: National Museum of American History, Smithsonian Institution

PRICE 25 CENTS.

OFFICIAL PROGRAMME INAUGURAL CEREMONIES

Washington D.C.

MARCH 4TH

1897

Lauding "the manlier virtues" in his 1905 inaugural address, and urging his fellow citizens to embrace "courage, hardihood, and endurance," Theodore Roosevelt—the Spanish-American war hero who compared his strength to that of a bull moose—personified the swaggering optimism Americans felt about the young century. TR's was also the first inauguration to feature the automobile, a 19th-century invention that would become a symbol of personal freedom and technological innovation in the 20th century. However, it wouldn't be until Warren Harding in 1921 that a president would actually ride from the Capitol to the White House in a horseless carriage on inauguration day.

Photographs: National Museum of American History, Smithsonian Institution

Fellow Republicans Calvin Coolidge and Herbert Hoover, the outgoing and incoming presidents, ride together from the White House to Capitol Hill for Hoover's inauguration on March 4, 1929 (*below*). The pair are the only two presidents to have been sworn into office by an ex-president: William Howard Taft, who served as the Chief Justice of the United States after leaving the White House. The Chief Justice has led the president in the oath of office since the early days of the Republic. The first inauguration of Woodrow Wilson, who succeeded Taft as president, was note-worthy for the 8,000 women's suffragists who briefly blocked his route from the White House to the Capitol. It was during Wilson's second term, in 1920, that the 19th Amendment to the Constitution was passed, giving women nationwide the right to vote. Neither men nor women residing in the District of Columbia, however, would be allowed to vote in a presidential election until 1964.

Photographs: right, National Museum of American History, Smithsonian Institution; below, Library of Congress

Four times inaugurated, Franklin Delano Roosevelt used the occasion of his first inauguration (*above*) to utter one of the most memorable lines in the history of American politics, reassuring a nation panicked by the Great Depression that "the only thing we have to fear is fear itself." That address, on March 4, 1933, marked the last March inauguration: the 20th Amendment to the Constitution moved the ceremony to January 20 beginning in 1937, in order to reduce the time between the presidential election and the winner taking office. An unintended benefit surfaced when researchers reported that the weather in Washington has historically been finer on January 20 than on March 4.

Photographs: right, Eric F. Long;
all, National Museum of American History,
Smithsonian Institution

The first president born in the 20th century, John Fitzgerald Kennedy shows off his famed vigor by standing hatless in the chill wind (*left*) to exhort listeners to his inaugural address in 1961 to "ask not what your country can do for you: ask what you can do for your country." Less than three years after President Kennedy's inaugural parade (*below*), a far more somber mood prevailed as Lyndon Johnson took the oath of office on Air Force One, the presidential plane (*lower left*), following President Kennedy's assassination in Dallas.

Photographs: left and this page, National Museum of American History, Smithsonian Institution; lower left, Cecil Stoughton

Photograph: Robin Bowman

The festivities for 1997's inaugural weekend began in earnest on Friday, January 17. With Washington bedecked in bunting, and parties beginning all over town, a children's gospel choir rehearses at New Bethel Church of God in Christ under the guidance of Rickey Payton, Sr. (*above*). Less than 72 hours later, choir members Autumn Stevenson (*upper right*) and Ebony Hamilton (*lower right*) would be on the steps of the Capitol for the inaugural ceremony, as their group, Children of the Gospel: the Next Generation, performed for President Clinton, Vice President Gore, and a worldwide television audience.

Photographs: Pete Souza

There hasn't been an inaugural parade
without floats since the first ones appeared
in William Henry Harrison's parade in
1841. Peter Epstein (*above*) puts the final
touches on a depiction of the American
eagle for the 1997 parade; other floats
featured the Church of Jesus Christ of
Latter-day Saints, the Holy Cross Gospel
Choir of Rhode Island, and the Wisconsin
Polka Hall of Fame, among others.

Photographs: Mark Abraham

Following page: A fireworks specialist from the Grucci Family readies the goodies for Saturday evening's outdoor extravaganza. The Gruccis are the only entertainment group to have taken part in seven consecutive inaugurations.

Photograph: Pete Souza

On Saturday and Sunday myriad activities made up "An American Journey" (*left*), a public festival held on the Mall, the grassy expanse that runs west from the Capitol and links many of Washington's most treasured monuments and museums. The food was eclectic, the talent abundant, and the tents heated—much to the relief of the thousands who braved sharp winds and temperatures in the low 20s to take part in the free events. The purpose, according to Inaugural Committee co-chair Ann Dibble Jordan, was to celebrate America's "strength, spirit and community." Visitors took the opportunity to post messages (*above*) for President Clinton and Vice President Gore, in answer to the question "How Would You Build a Bridge to the 21st Century?"

Photographs: left, David Burnett; above, Ron Haviv

The curious peek inside the Technology Playground (*left*), where a young surfer checks out the World Wide Web (*above*). The 1997 inaugural ceremony was the first to be broadcast in real time over the Internet, and the 1997 Inaugural Committee was the first to have a home page on the Web. Other noted technology breakthroughs in inaugural history include the first telegraph report (James Polk, 1845); the first public address system (Harding, 1921); the first radio broadcast of an inaugural address (Coolidge, 1925); and the first television broadcast (Truman, 1949).

Photographs: left, Olivier Laude; above, Martin Simon

The festival's Heritage Hall hosts members
of the Foxwoods Dance Troupe on Sunday
morning (*above and right*). The first Native
Americans to have a formal part in an
inauguration were several tribal leaders
who rode in Theodore Roosevelt's 1905
parade (*upper right*). Identified with a
hand-written note scrawled on the back
of the photo, they are, left to right, "Little
Plume, chief of the Nez Perce; Buckskin
Charlie, chief of the Utes; Geronimo,
Apache warrior; Quanah Parker, chief of
the Comanche; Hollow Horn Bear, Sioux
chief; and American Horse, Sioux Indian."

Photographs: above and right, Paul Fusco;
upper right, National Museum of American
History, Smithsonian Institution

Because the inaugural festivities coincided with the annual holiday set aside to mark the birth of Dr. Martin Luther King, Jr., a rare performance of the musical "King!" graced the stage of Heritage Hall on Sunday afternoon (*left*). The show's producer, Albert Nellum, and its lyricist, Maya Angelou (*above*), watch their work being performed with Angelou's original script and libretto for the first time since she withdrew her support from the show's 1990 debut production in London. This performance marked the show's premiere in the United States. Angelou wrote and recited the poem "On the Pulse of Morning" at President Clinton's first inauguration.

Photographs: Paul Fusco

Photograph: Robin Bowman

Young revelers were drawn to the musical tents (*below and right*), which shook to the sounds of various performers including Better than Ezra, Celtic Thunder, Chaka Khan, Little Feat, Eddie Palmieri, The Count Basie Orchestra, Nashville Bluegrass, Peter Paul & Mary, Buckwheat Zydeco, and former Grateful Dead member Bob Weir. Barney and Elmo were on hand for the younger set, and James Whitmore performed his one-man show as Will Rogers. But there was more than fun and games. With the help of the Smithsonian Institution and the Holocaust Museum, speakers such as Betty Friedan, Elie Weisel, Ken Burns, and T. Berry Brazelton discussed America's past and future.

Photographs: below, Paul Fusco; right, Ron Haviv

Following page: Al Gore, by all accounts the most active vice president in U.S. history, greets members of the Young Marines in the Technology Playground. Members of the group of future military leaders served as ushers in the crowded tent, and also helped with security across the city over inaugural weekend. Gore himself spent time in uniform, serving in Vietnam with the Army's 20th Engineering Battalion.

Photograph: Robin Bowman

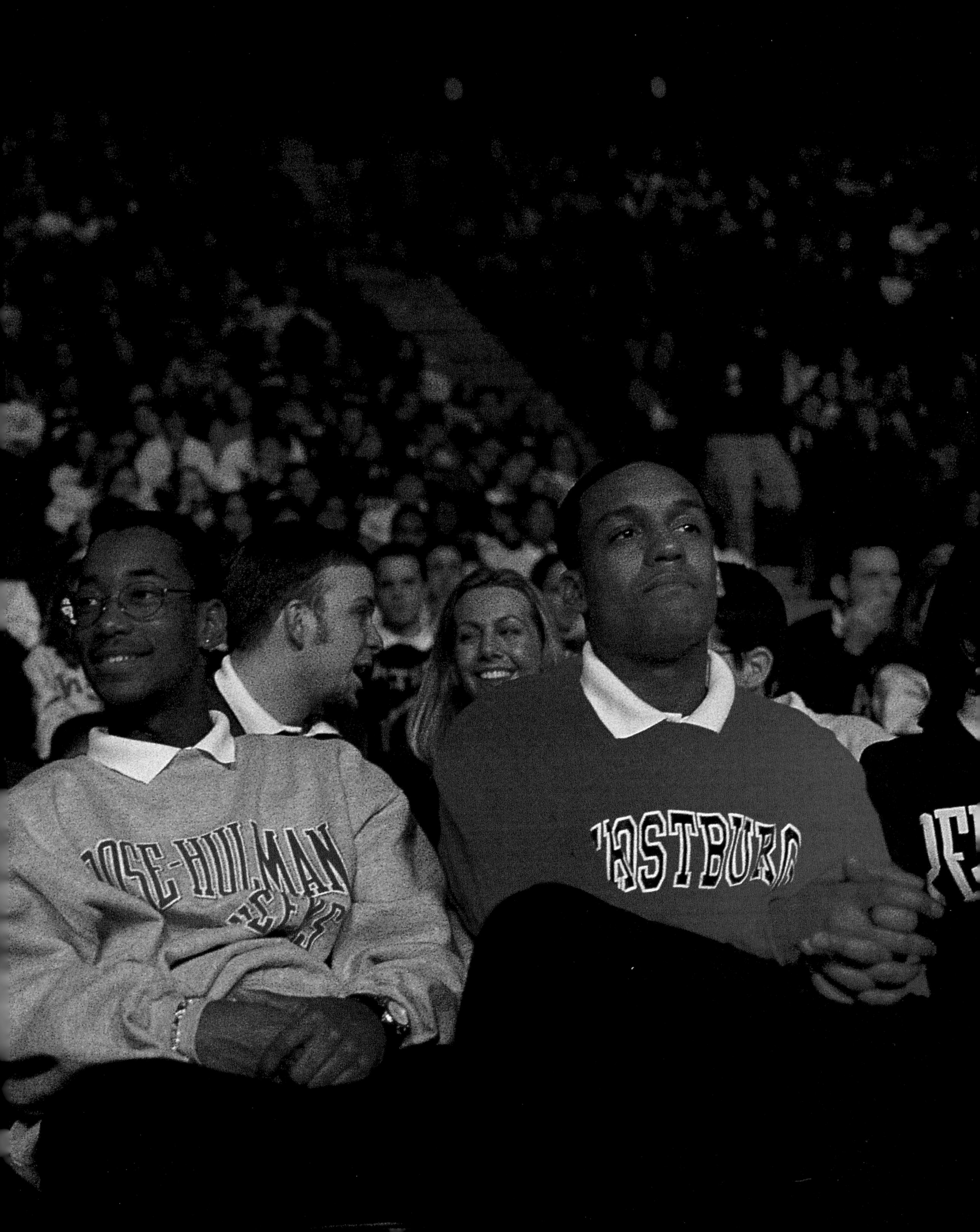

Previous page: First-year college students now, these four members of the Class of 2000, a singing group made up of college students from the D.C. area, represent the last group of collegians who will graduate in the 20th century. After their performance, they watch the other entertainers at the American Gala, the technical run-through of the next night's Presidential Gala.

Photograph: Ed Kashi

Admission to the American Gala, held Saturday night at the US Air Arena, was a can of food to be donated to area food banks. Many of the stars in the line-up for Sunday's black-tie Presidential Gala also performed at the American Gala, where the crowd of about 12,000—standing for the United States Marine Drum and Bugle Corps' rendition of the Star-Spangled Banner (*left and above*)—favored casual attire.

Photographs: upper left, Ed Kashi; lower left and above, Ron Haviv

45

At a luncheon in their honor, members of
an elite American club pose for a group
portrait. All earned a Congressional Medal
of Honor, the country's highest award for
bravery, by performing acts of courage
above and beyond the call of duty in battle.
Fewer than a thousand medals have been
awarded in this century. The honored
veterans enjoyed a full schedule over the
weekend, with a whirlwind of receptions,
VIP seating at the swearing-in and parade,
attendance at the "Salute to Heroes"
inaugural ball, and a wreath laying at
the Tomb of the Unknowns at Arlington
National Cemetery. Military units (*right,*
at James Garfield's parade in 1881) have
been a lynchpin of inaugural celebrations
for two centuries.

Photographs: below, Ed Kashi;
right, Architect of the Capitol

A dream deferred finally realized:
Lieutenant Vernon Baker received a
Congressional Medal of Honor in 1996, five
decades after leading a 25-man battalion as
it destroyed six German machine gun nests,
two observer posts and four dugouts in Italy.
More than a million African-American
soldiers fought for their country in World
War II, but none was granted the Medal of
Honor until Baker and six others were
chosen; in the years following the war, any
recommendations for Medals of Honor for
black soldiers were systematically destroyed.
The six other combatants all fell in battle,
making Baker the nation's only living
African-American recipient of a Medal
of Honor earned during World War II.

Photograph: Ed Kashi

47

In the church where Martin Luther King, Jr., delivered his last sermon, Wynton Marsalis and his septet present a concert entitled "In This House On This Morning" to honor his memory. The soaring Gothic church, Washington National Cathedral, brims with presidential history: Theodore Roosevelt presided at groundbreaking ceremonies in 1907, holding the same trowel George Washington used to lay the cornerstone for the Capitol building; Woodrow Wilson's tomb is in the cathedral; and funeral services for both Wilson and Dwight Eisenhower were held here.

Photographs: Pete Souza

The King celebrations continued on January 19, four days after the Nobel Peace Prize–winning civil rights leader would have turned 68 years old. The 1997 Gospel Music Extravaganza stirred the audience at the Anna Johenning Baptist Church, with nationally renowned singers as well as local Washington choirs.

Photographs: Ed Kashi

Although the Presidential Inaugural Committee sponsored fourteen official inaugural balls, dozens of organizations and individuals held their own "unofficial" balls, parties, and galas throughout the Washington area on inaugural weekend. Dancing and toasting were on the agendas of both the Women's Inaugural Ball (*right*), sponsored by the National Women's Political Caucus, and the Women's Inaugural Gala (*above*), whose host committee included People for the American Way. Women who supported Bill Clinton and Al Gore in 1996 had a lot to celebrate: the Democratic ticket carried 54% of the women's vote; Bob Dole captured only 37%, with 7% going to Ross Perot.

Photographs: Najlah Feanny

A somewhat unlikely player on the national
political scene, the MTV cable network feted
the inauguration with a party at Washington's
Corcoran Gallery of Art (*above*), around the
corner from the White House. MTV exploded
into the consciousness of campaign managers
after candidate Clinton appeared on the
network in 1992. Diva Zappa, daughter of
the late musician Frank Zappa, was tied up
in knots for the party (*right*), which was
co-hosted by Condé-Nast.

Photographs: Mark Peterson

53

More than 2,000 fiesta lovers spent
Saturday evening at Union Station, the
only retail center in Washington that is
also a working train depot, for the Hispanic
Ball, hosted by Congress's Hispanic
Caucus. The growing political clout of
Hispanic-Americans was underscored by
appearances at the ball by Vice President
Gore and First Lady Hillary Rodham
Clinton. Entertainment included the
dance troupe La Mafia (*right*).

Photograph: Mannie Garcia

"Our rich texture of racial, religious, and political diversity," President Clinton would say in his inaugural address on Monday, "will be a Godsend in the 21st century." The diversity was on display at gatherings throughout the weekend, including the Historic Asian Pacific American Inaugural Ball (*right*), where the political figures mingling with the crowd included Leon Panetta, President Clinton's former chief of staff, and Gary Locke, the governor of Washington who is the first Asian-American elected to that post in any state. A few blocks away revelers enjoyed the Black and White Ball (*below*), sponsored by a group of D.C. residents originally from North Carolina.

Photographs: below, Mark Peterson; upper and lower right, Robin Bowman

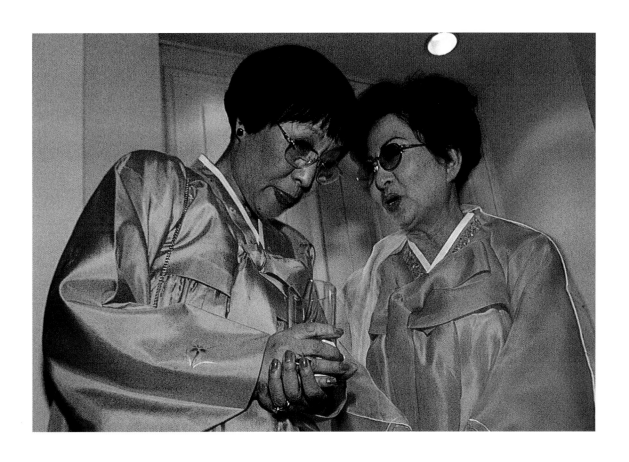

Her business card introduces her as a "Positive Thinker, Volunteer, Fund Raiser, Perpetual Cheerleader & Mad Hatter." And that's not all: Willie Oates (*left*) is also a proud resident of the state of Arkansas, where Bill Clinton served for twelve years as governor before moving onto the national stage. At the Blue Jeans Bash on Friday night, Oates joined the Young Arkansas Democrats in nibbling on Southern food as the band Little Feat entertained the crowd.

The next night, another celebration in honor of the president was hosted by the Clinton Birthplace Foundation (*above*). Proceeds from the party—where musical entertainment included the Platters, the Drifters, the Coasters and the Marvellettes—are earmarked to restore the president's boyhood home.

Photographs: left, Sam Kittner; above, Olivier Laude

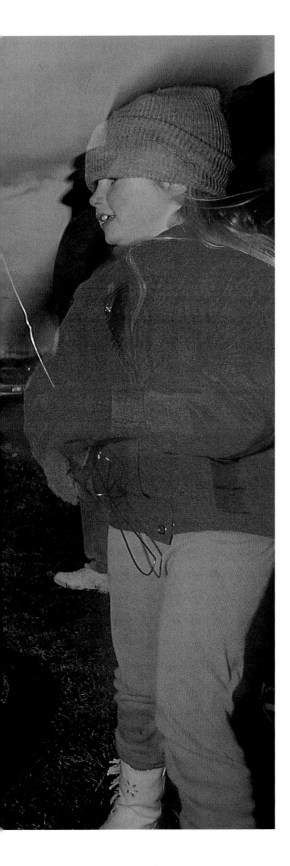

Waiting for the most ambitious fireworks show in Washington's history to begin Saturday evening, the Flynn family (from left to right: Mike, Mike, Jr., Tim, and Lauren) allow passers-by to share their fire's warmth. The cold was a hassle but not a hindrance all weekend (*above*), and those who found a clear and warm place to watch the fireworks were amply rewarded. The show, "Sharing the Light," was the handiwork of a family business on Long Island, Fireworks by Grucci, which launched the simultaneous, synchronized displays from ten locations around Washington.

Photographs: left, Sam Kittner; above, Mark Peterson

Photograph: David Burnett

Photographs: David Burnett

Soon after the entrances of the First Family
and Vice President and Mrs. Gore (*right*)
at Sunday evening's Presidential Gala, fan
dancers from the cast of the Broadway
musical "Chicago" (*above*) delight the
crowd.

Photographs: Rick Rickman

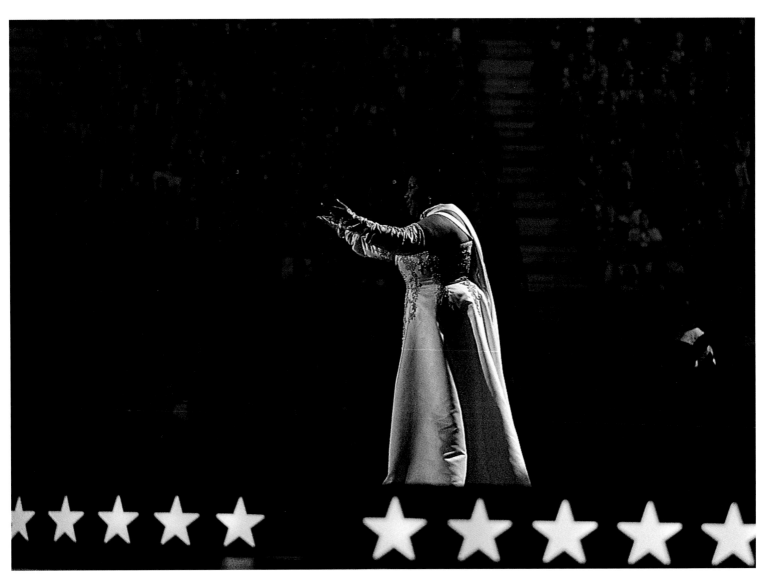

The queen of soul, Aretha Franklin, emotes for the president at the Gala (*upper left*), where formal wear was *de rigueur* (*lower left*). Tickets ranged from $100 to $3,000 in price, with those lucky enough to have front-row seats getting a handshake from the president after the show (*above*). The star-studded Gala was nationally televised later that night on CBS.

Photographs: Rick Rickman

70

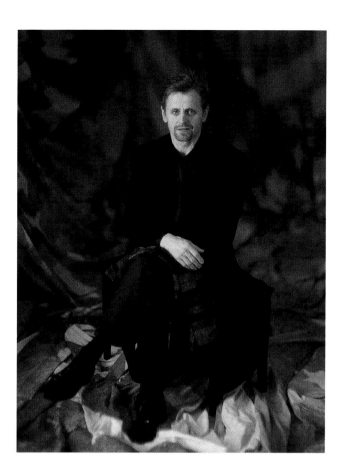

Among the talent performing at the
Presidential Gala were (*clockwise from top
left*) Gloria Estefan; Kenny Rogers; Aretha
Franklin; Mikhail Baryshnikov; Raymond
Pound, Ralph Armstrong, and Rudolph
Standfield (Aretha's back-up band); Bernadette
Peters; and Stevie Wonder. Other celebrities on
stage at the Gala included Candice Bergen,
Michael Douglas, Kenny G, Whoopi Goldberg,
Jimmy Smits, James Taylor, and Yo-Yo Ma.
More traditional patriotic fare was handled by
the United States Armed Forces Color Team,
the United States Army Herald Trumpets, the
United States Army Drill Team, the United
States Marine Drum and Bugle Corps, and the
United States Naval Academy Glee Club.

Photographs: Gregory Heisler

Photograph: Galen Rowell

It's the calm before the crowd for ushers at the Capitol (*above*), where the president was scheduled to be sworn in precisely at noon. In the afternoon, the Clintons would travel along Pennsylvania Avenue from the Capitol to the White House, kicking off the inaugural parade. In dawn's chill, security forces take a final walk of the parade route (*right*), where manhole covers will be lifted and the manholes explored by specially trained dogs in order to ward off any mischief.

Photographs: above, Mannie Garcia; right, Robin Bowman

The Clintons and Gores begin inauguration day at the National Prayer Service, held at the Metropolitan African Methodist Episcopal (AME) Church a few blocks from the White House. The thirteen religious leaders and eleven musical participants contributing to the ecumenical service include Jesse Jackson and soloist Mickey Mangun (*left*). The crowd of friends, family, and church members joining the First Family at the 8 A.M. service included D.C. Board of Education member Wilma Harvey (*below, to Mrs. Clinton's right*), the sister of the Metropolitan AME's host pastor, Reverend Louis-Charles Harvey. The church made history in 1993 when it became the first predominantly African-American church to host the National Prayer Service.

Photographs: Sam Kittner

A crowd of about 200,000 assembles on the Mall (*right*) to witness the inaugural ceremonies, under the watchful eye of, among others, the Statue of Freedom (*above*) atop the Capitol dome. As the crowd gathered, the president prepared to ride to the Capitol in a limousine with senators John Warner and Wendell Ford, members of the Joint Congressional Committee on Inaugural Ceremonies, and Speaker of the House Newt Gingrich.

Photographs: above, Kylen Campbell; right, Martin Simon

Chelsea Clinton shares a smile before
the swearing-in with the vice president's
children: Kristin, Karenna, Sarah, and
Albert III (*left*). The inauguration of the
head of the government's executive branch,
an event held on the steps of the home of
the legislative branch, is made complete
by the presence of the judicial branch:
members of the U.S. Supreme Court
(*above*). The black skullcaps justices now
wear at occasions of state were introduced
at Woodrow Wilson's inauguration;
previous to that date, justices wore top
hats at outdoor events.

Photographs: David Burnett

Opera diva Jessye Norman accepts the
crowd's kudos after her "American Medley"
(*below*). The rehearsals of Children of the
Gospel: the Next Generation (see page 22)
paid off, as the group performs "Let's Build
a Bridge Across America" (*right*). Poet
Miller Williams added to the ceremony's
artistic touch, reading a poem he wrote
especially for the inauguration.

Photographs: Mannie Garcia

Albert Gore, Jr., takes the oath of office of vice president from U.S. Supreme Court Associate Justice Ruth Bader Ginsburg, surrounded by his wife and children. The vice president's father, respected Tennessee lawmaker Albert Gore, Sr., served three terms as a senator and once had presidential aspirations himself.

Photographs: below, Galen Rowell; right, Gregory Heisler

Following page: At five minutes past noon on January 20, 1997, William Jefferson Clinton became the youngest man inaugurated to a second term after serving a full first term as president. With his hand on a Bible open to Isaiah 58:12, the fifty-year-old Clinton takes the oath from William Rehnquist, Chief Justice of the United States. Among the government officials standing nearby are House Majority Leader Dick Armey, Speaker of the House Newt Gingrich, Senate Majority Leader Trent Lott, House Democratic Leader Richard Gephardt, Vice President Gore, Senator John Warner, and Senator Wendell Ford.

Photograph: Mannie Garcia

"We began the 19th century with a choice, to spread our nation from coast to coast," President Clinton said in his inaugural address (*right*). "We began the 20th century with a choice, to harness the Industrial Revolution to our values of free enterprise, conservation, and human decency." And now, he added, "At the dawn of the 21st century a free people must now choose to shape the forces of the Information Age and the global society, to unleash the limitless potential of all our people." Abraham Lincoln delivered his own second inaugural speech (*above*) only a month before the end of the Civil War, urging Americans to approach reconstruction "with malice toward none, with charity for all, with firmness in the right as God gives us to see the right . . . ." Echoing this spirit of hope a century later, President Clinton reminded his audience that "there is much to dare. The demands of our time are great and they are different. Let us meet them with faith and courage, with patience and a grateful and happy heart. Let us build our bridge."

Photographs: above, National Archives; right, Acey Harper

Previous page: All eyes are on the
president as he delivers his inaugural
address from the West Front of the Capitol.
Most inaugurations were held on the East
Front until 1981, when Ronald Reagan
began his first term as president. Because
the West Front allows more spectators to
be seated more comfortably, Reagan's
successors have also chosen it as the
launching point for their administrations.

Photograph: Gregory Heisler

After delivering his 22-minute speech—longer than Washington's second, which was all of 135 words, but shorter than William Henry Harrison's two-hour stemwinder—President Clinton shakes a few hands (*left*) before entering the Capitol. Inside, he signs the the first executive order of his new term to the applause of Vice President Gore and key Congressional leaders (*below*). He then moved to Statuary Hall for the traditional lunch with members of Congress. The menu, taken from an 1838 collection of recipes from Thomas Jefferson's home, featured shrimp, oyster and scallop pie, beef a la mode, beggar's pudding and quince ice cream.

Photographs: left, Mannie Garcia, below, Callie Shell

94

VCR 1   VCR 2

VCR 3   VCR 4

It may look like a TV junkie's dream, but these are no ordinary couch potatoes. At the Joint Operation Center in the Washington suburbs, representatives of the FBI, the Federal Emergency Management System, local police and fire jurisdictions, and the military study ten television feeds of the inaugural parade (*left*), eyes flitting back and forth just like Secret Service agents in the field. The center was the work of the Armed Forces Inaugural Committee, a task force designed to coordinate the military's support for the events of inaugural weekend. During the parade, a sniper patrol (*above*) stands guard atop the Old Executive Office Building, the sprawling 19th-century, Gothic-style building next to the White House.

Photographs: left, Sam Kittner; above, Barbara Ries

The view of the inaugural parade through the bleachers has its limits, but it still offers a slice of history. The first inaugural parade, in 1805, was an impromptu affair, when a group of giddy Washingtonians fell in behind Thomas Jefferson as he walked from the young Capitol to the president's house after taking the oath for the second time. By the time of Woodrow Wilson's first inauguration in 1913, there were 40,000 participants in the march down Pennsylvania Avenue—a record that has never been equaled. This year, some 6,000 marchers, representing all fifty states as well as the U.S. territories, covered the route, which is about a mile and a half.

Photograph: below, David Burnett; right, David Alan Harvey

Following page: A wedge of motorcycle police heralds the parade's beginning, with the presidential limousine not far behind. The red-and-white flag of the District of Columbia flies beside Old Glory along the avenue.

Photograph: Galen Rowell

About one-third of 1997's parade participants marched in military units. Perhaps there's a 21st-century president among those in uniform: history shows that one future Commander-in-Chief, Dwight Eisenhower, took part in an inaugural parade as a young man, stepping off in Woodrow Wilson's 1913 parade forty years before his own.

Photographs: upper left, Ed Kashi; lower left, Barbara Ries; above, Olivier Laude

Hey, Mr. Vice President, up here! Rooftops along Pennsylvania Avenue are prime parade real estate: companies with offices along the parade route often host inauguration day parties, and hotel rooms with windows looking out on Pennsylvania Avenue are booked for inauguration day years in advance. The group (*above*) wishing Clinton good luck—*buena suerte*—underscores the support the Democratic ticket received from Hispanic voters, 72% of whom voted for Clinton-Gore.

Photographs: top and right, Martin Simon; above, Rick Rickman

Following page: the First Family walks the last block of the parade route, in a reprise of the stroll the president and First Lady took in 1993. Jimmy and Rosalynn Carter walked the entire parade route in 1977, in a move designed to win back public trust in the presidency, which had been shattered by Watergate and the subsequent resignation of President Nixon in 1974.

Photograph: Barbara Kinney

The Florida A&M band struts its stuff in front of the presidential viewing stand. Each president puts his personal stamp on his viewing stand; President Clinton chose to follow the design originally created for John F. Kennedy (*above*) by architect Robert Brackett. JFK's handwritten note to Brackett said "A beautiful design—but where is the snow?" in reference to the chilly weather the crowds endured that day. Kennedy's inaugural parade also led to more permanent changes in Washington architecture. The president was reportedly concerned by the dowdy state of Pennsylvania Avenue as he traveled from the Capitol to the White House, and his interest sparked the Avenue's eventual redevelopment. The face-lift of the Kennedy years extended to the White House, where First Lady Jacqueline Kennedy presided over a detailed and historically precise restoration of the interior. The exterior has undergone three significant alterations since John Adams became the first occupant in 1800: the front portico was appended in 1829, the wings attached in 1902, and—perhaps most importantly—the Virginia sandstone exterior was painted white to cover up smoke damage caused by British bombardments during the War of 1812. From then on, the building originally called the President's Palace, or President's Mansion, has been known the world over as the White House.

Photographs: left, Barbara Ries; above, National Museum of American History, Smithsonian Institution

While Chelsea Clinton watches the parade with her young cousin, Zachary Rodham, and aunt, Nicole Boxer Rodham (*left*), the president waves from behind the glass partition. The U.S. Army band (*right*) was one of more than two dozen to march in the parade, most representing high schools, colleges, and universities. In addition, eleven other bands stood on street corners along the parade route and entertained the spectators—many of whom staked out their spots in the early morning—before the parade finally got underway more than an hour after its scheduled start time of 2:00 P.M.

Photographs: left, Barbara Ries; below and right, Ed Kashi

The flashy Florida A&M band (*upper left*) and the musicians offering Southwestern music from their float (*lower left*) were among many diverse performers giving a distinctly multicultural cast to the parade. There was even, as evidenced by the Republican elephants on one spectator's hat (*above*), a bipartisan cast. House Speaker Newt Gingrich, a Republican who sparred with President Clinton during his first term at the White House, called the day a "joyous occasion." In presenting President Clinton and Vice President Gore with the flags that had flown over the Capitol at 7 A.M. on inauguration day, he said, "We cherish and wish you Godspeed in your administration," adding that "this capacity to transfer power . . . is truly one of the miraculous events of the planet."

Photographs: upper and lower left, Olivier Laude; above, Paul Fusco

Many still in fighting trim, members of the Veterans of Foreign Wars march proudly for a grateful nation (*above*). All of the president's official honor guard (*right*), nicknamed the Old Guard, are in fighting trim, and then some: members must be at least six feet tall and have a maximum waist measurement of thirty inches. Requirements are less stringent for the Colorado-based Living History Association, whose members preserve memories of the past by donning uniforms such as those worn by drummer boys in the Civil War (*far right*).

Photographs: above, Karen Kasmauski; right and far right, Leif Skoogfors

The First Lady and First Daughter applaud the president at one of the fourteen official inaugural balls scattered around Washington on the evening of January 20 (*left*). The festivities at all fourteen— thirteen regional balls and one youth ball— included at least a brief appearance by both the Gores and the president and Mrs. Clinton. All were open to the public, with tickets selling for $150 each. President Dwight Eisenhower (*above,* with wife, Mamie, son, John, and daughter-in-law, Barbara) was the guest of honor at two official balls in 1953 and four in 1957, making him the first president in years to have more than one formal ball and starting a trend that led to 1997's record number of dances.

Photographs: left, David Burnett; above, Washington Post

The president left his saxophone at home, but there was still music galore at the balls—including sets by Marcus Davis (*below*), Bo Diddley (*upper right*) and Kenny G (*lower right*). Diddley shared the stage at the Mid-Atlantic States Ball with fellow rock and blues legends Chuck Berry and John Mayall. In addition to the headliners, lesser-known acts were booked from all over America, according to Director of Talent Bobbie Faye Ferguson, in order to make the events a more inclusive, national celebration.

Photographs: below, Jason Miccolo Johnson; upper right, Rick Rickman; lower right, Robin Bowman

117

It was a night for the young and energetic, from the official DC Ball (*above*) to the party sponsored by the Close Up Foundation in Alexandria, Virginia, just south of Washington (*right*). The foundation encourages the political and public service aspirations of the best and brightest of America's high school students. Back in Washington, the Postal Square Museum hosted the 21st Century Ball, an official inaugural ball for young people with ticket prices of only $50.

Photographs: above, David Alan Harvey; right, Sam Kittner

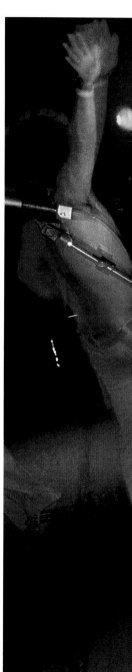

Following page: A proud father takes to the dance floor with the First Lady at—where else?—the Arkansas Ball, one of three balls held simultaneously at the Washington Convention Center.

Photographs: left, David Burnett, right, Sharon Farmer

Just as presidential inaugurations are for lovers of democracy, inaugural balls are for just plain lovers, from the famous (*right*) to the anonymous (*below*). If these slow-dancers know the steps of the cotillion or the minuet, they were keeping it under wraps—unlike newly-inaugurated President George Washington, who is said to have danced both at a New York City reception in his honor in 1789. The first inaugural ball held in Washington was probably James Madison's in 1809, hosted by the then-fashionable Long's Hotel on Capitol Hill and attended by 400 people.

Photographs: below, David Alan Harvey; right, Najlah Feanny

Following page: The vice president and Mrs. Gore, and the First Family, in portraits made backstage at the Arkansas Ball especially for this book.

Photographs: Gregory Heisler

The 53rd Presidential Inaugural Committee

General Co-Chairs

Ann Dibble Jordan
Terence R. McAuliffe

Honorary Chairs

The Honorable Christopher Dodd
The Honorable Ann Richards
The Honorable Don Fowler

Vice Chairs

Ron Burkle
Linda Chavez-Thompson
The Honorable Lawton Chiles
Beth Dozoretz
Gordon Giffin
Robert Johnson
Ellen Malcolm
Richard Mays
Carol Pensky
The Honorable Edward Rendell
Ed Romero
Elaine Schuster
Fred Seigel
Stanley Shuman
Mary Elizabeth Teasley
Jonathan Tisch

Co-Executive Directors

Debbie Willhite
Craig T. Smith

Executive Producer

Harry Thomason

		ARMED FORCES INAUGURAL COMMITTEE	
Finance Chairman	Daniel A. Dutko		
Senior Advisor to the Co-Chairs	Laura Hartigan	*Chairman*	Major General Robert F. Foley United States Army
Deputy Co-Executive Director	Kathy Webb	*Deputy Chairman*	Brigadier General Charles R. Viale United States Army
Assistants to the Co-Chairs	Kelly Green Jason McIntosh	*Chief of Staff*	Colonel James W. Hust United States Marine Corps
General Counsel	Deborah Ashford		
Chief Counsel	Ken Stern	JOINT CONGRESSIONAL COMMITTEE ON INAUGURAL	
Chief Financial Officer	Brad Marshall	CEREMONIES	Honorable John W. Warner
Director of Revenue	Bradley Kiley		Honorable Trent Lott
Comptroller	Jeffrey C. King		Honorable Wendell Ford
			Honorable Newt Gingrich
			Honorable Richard A. Gephardt
		Executive Director	Susan Magill

FINANCE
Directors   Joan F. Kenny
                       Kristopher M. Van Giesen

OFFICE OF THE VICE PRESIDENT
Director   Winston McGregor
Deputy Director   Laura Segal

ADMINISTRATION/OPERATIONS
Director   Amed Khan
Deputy Directors   Edward Ertal
                       Karen Weigert

COMMUNICATIONS
Director   Craig Sutherland
Inaugural Spokesperson Kiki Moore

DESIGN, GRAPHICS AND PRODUCTION
                       Robert Mele
                       John Pastore
                       Virginia Fleischman

EVENTS
Director   Stacie Spector
Deputy Director   Nancy Ozeas

INAUGURAL BALLS
Director   Elaine Howard
Deputy Director   Seth Robinson

INAUGURAL GALA
Director   Jill Alper
Deputy Director for Site Paul Thomas Rivera
Deputy Director for   Eric K. Sildon
  Operations
Deputy Director for   Billy Sparks
  Administration

MARKETING
Director   Robert L. Mallett
Deputy Director   Argelia Rodriguez

MALL EVENTS
Co-Directors   Morris Reid
                       Rebecca McKenzie
Deputy Director for   Jennifer Curley
  Outreach
Deputy Director for   Atif Harden
  Administration
Deputy Director for Site Adam Sitkoff

MEDIA LOGISTICS
Director   Edward Emerson
Deputy Director   Oriella Ben-Zvi

PARADE
Director   Jeff Forbes
Deputy Director   Sarah Farnsworth

POLITICAL OUTREACH
Director   Ertharin Cousin
Deputy Director   Cynthia Jasso-Rotunno

PRAYER SERVICE
Director   Brian Gallagher

SCHEDULING/ADVANCE
Director   Janna Sidley
Deputy Director   Aviva Steinberg

TALENT
Director   Bobbie Faye Ferguson
Deputy Director   Michelle Day

TICKETING
Director   Kim Cubine
Deputies to the Director Christopher Gruin
                       Christine Kenngott
                       Sandy Thurman

VIPS
Co-Directors   Fred DuVal
                       Sylvia Panetta
Deputy Director   Rod O'Conner

VOLUNTEERS
Director   Ana Ramirez
Deputies to the Director Alex Matthiessen
                       Jaime Uzeta

Special Assistants
  Dana Adams   Alex Mandi
  Jason Bovis   Mike McNamara
  Michael Coen   Jodie Moxley
  Donald Dunn   Abby Nachtom
  Elizabeth Fleming   Whitney Staley
  Christopher Lavery   Matt Twist

GENERAL SERVICES ADMINISTRATION
  INAUGURAL STAFF
Chief Operating Officer   Joel Odum
Deputy Chief Operating Pamela Berry
  Officer

UNITED STATES SENATE
Majority Leader   The Honorable Trent Lott
Democratic Leader The Honorable Tom Daschle

UNITED STATES HOUSE OF REPRESENTATIVES
Speaker   The Honorable Newt Gingrich
Majority Leader   The Honorable Richard Armey
Democratic Leader The Honorable Richard A.
                         Gephardt

ABOUT THIS BOOK . . .

THE PHOTOGRAPHS IN *AN AMERICAN JOURNEY* WERE CREATED BY 25 PHOTOJOURNALISTS
SHOOTING NEARLY 1,000 ROLLS OF FILM OVER THE FOUR DAYS OF INAUGURAL EVENTS.
ALL PHOTOGRAPHS WERE MADE WITH THE MOST ADVANCED PROFESSIONAL FILM AVAILABLE:
KODAK EKTACHROME EL100, KODACHROME KR64, AND KODACHROME KL200.
HISTORICAL OBJECTS WERE PHOTOGRAPHED ON KODAK EKTACHROME ESW100 FILM.
THE TOTAL TAKE OF ALMOST 35,000 FRAMES WAS THEN EDITED DOWN TO 400 TOP SELECTS.
THESE IMAGES WERE SCANNED ONTO KODAK PHOTO CD
VIA A KODAK PHOTO CD IMAGING WORKSTATION,
AND IMPORTED INTO QUARKXPRESS 3.3 FOR LAYOUT ON POWER MACINTOSH 9500/120 COMPUTERS.
THE BOOK WAS DELIVERED TO THE PRINTER 28 DAYS AFTER THE INAUGURATION.

FOUR-COLOR SEPARATIONS AND PRINTING WERE DONE BY
RR DONNELLEY & SONS COMPANY, WILLARD, OHIO.

SPECIAL THANKS TO SABA PRESS PHOTOS FOR USE OF THEIR PHOTO EDITING FACILITIES,
AND TO HARRY RUBENSTEIN AND ALL THOSE AT THE NATIONAL MUSEUM OF AMERICAN HISTORY,
SMITHSONIAN INSTITUTION, WHO MADE THE HISTORICAL SECTION OF THIS BOOK POSSIBLE.

Photograph: Robin Bowman